COMPUTERS

Everyday Inventions

Kristin Petrie
ABDO Publishing Company

visit us at
www.abdopublishing.com

Published by ABDO Publishing Company, 8000 West 78th Street, Edina, Minnesota 55439. Copyright © 2009 by Abdo Consulting Group, Inc. International copyrights reserved in all countries. No part of this book may be reproduced in any form without written permission from the publisher. The Checkerboard Library™ is a trademark and logo of ABDO Publishing Company.

Printed in the United States.

Cover Photo: Getty Images
Interior Photos: Alamy pp. 18–19; AP Images p. 13; Corbis pp. 9, 10, 11, 12; Getty Images pp. 4, 5, 14, 16, 17, 24–25, 29; iStockphoto pp. 1, 15, 20, 22, 23; Photo Researchers p. 21; U.S. Department of Defense p. 27

Series Coordinator: Megan M. Gunderson
Editors: Rochelle Baltzer, Megan M. Gunderson
Art Direction & Cover Design: Neil Klinepier

Library of Congress Cataloging-in-Publication Data

Petrie, Kristin, 1970-
 Computers / Kristin Petrie.
     p. cm. -- (Everyday inventions)
 Includes index.
 ISBN 978-1-60453-086-5
 1. Computers--Juvenile literature. I. Title.

QA76.23.P48175 2009
004--dc22

2008001559

CONTENTS

Computers 4
Timeline 6
Computer Facts 7
Starting with ABC 8
Young Inventors 12
Bits and Pieces 14
Input and Output 20
Digital World 22
Networking 24
High-Tech Work 26
Computer Culture 28
Glossary 30
Web Sites 31
Index 32

Computers

Computers are everywhere! Today, these electronic devices continually store and process countless pieces of information.

But, the first computers were far simpler machines.

Do you know who invented the computer? Many people would like to take credit for this great success. But in truth, these machines are multiple inventions in one.

Many brilliant inventors put their ideas into the building of today's computers. In fact, you could even say they are still being invented. These devices improve daily!

Today, computers are a vital teaching tool. Many computer programs are educational and can be used at home or in school.

What do you do with computers? Do you chat with friends or search the World Wide Web? How about homework? Thanks to this invention, schoolwork goes a lot faster than it used to. Keep reading! You will be grateful for the amazing computer.

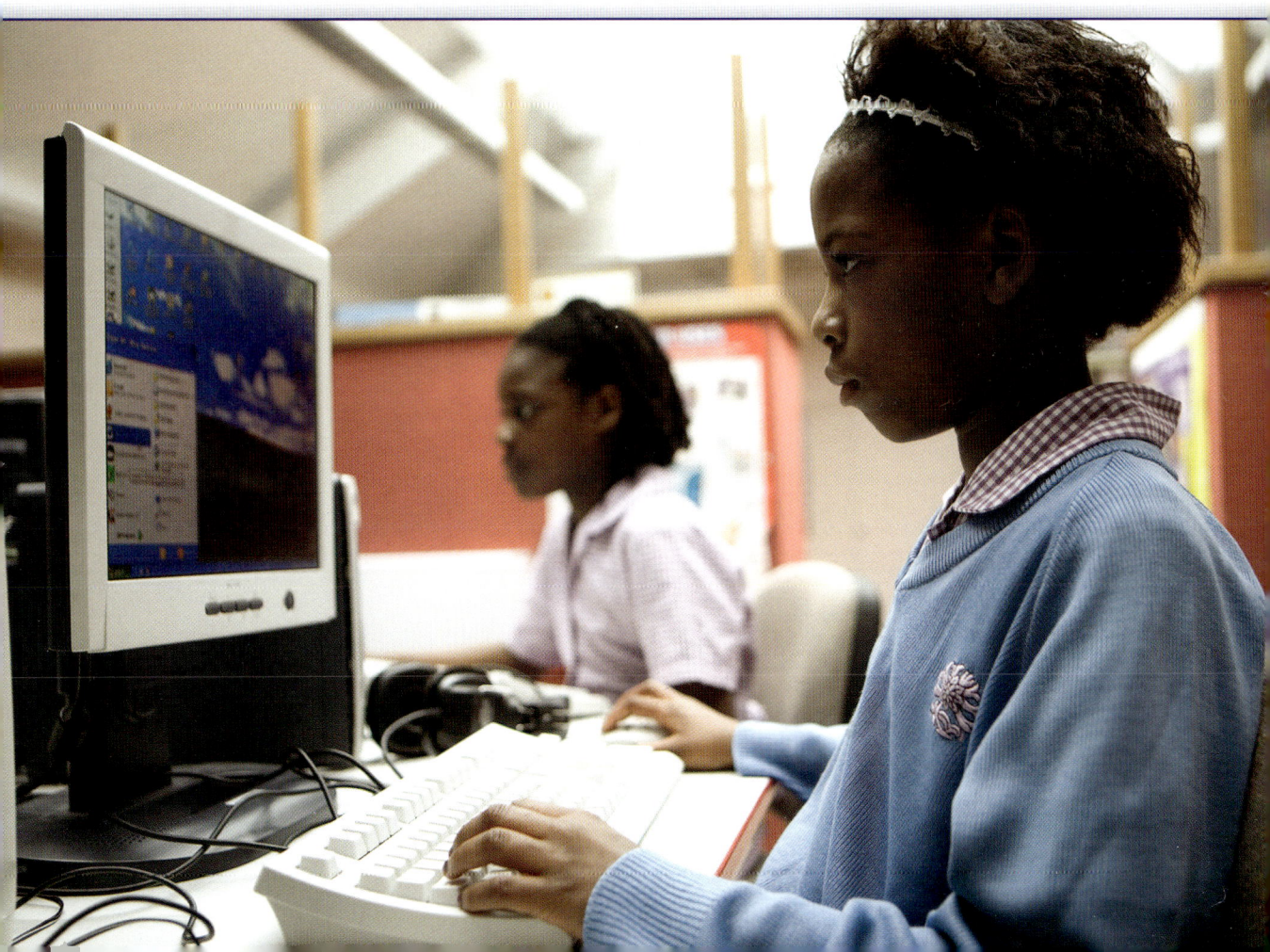

Timeline

1939	John V. Atanasoff and Clifford E. Berry built the Atanasoff-Berry Computer (ABC), the first electronic digital computer.
1944	The Harvard Mark I was revealed as the first automatic digital computer.
1945	The general-purpose Electronic Numerical Integrator and Computer (ENIAC) was built.
1951	Scientists presented the Electronic Discrete Variable Automatic Computer (EDVAC); the Universal Automatic Computer (UNIVAC) was invented.
1952	A UNIVAC was used to predict the U.S. presidential election.
1969	ARPANet connected government and university computers for the U.S. Department of Defense.
1975	William "Bill" Henry Gates III and Paul G. Allen cofounded Microsoft Corporation.
1976	Steven P. Jobs and Stephen G. Wozniak cofounded Apple Computer Inc.
1984	Apple created the Macintosh computer.
1991	The World Wide Web made the Internet more user-friendly.
1993	Internet browsers were introduced to make searching the Web easier.
2007	At 280.6 teraflops, IBM's BlueGene/L was named the world's fastest supercomputer.

Computer Facts

- The Inventors Hall of Fame in Akron, Ohio, recognizes inventors for their creativity and contributions to society. Apple Computer Inc. founder Stephen G. Wozniak was inducted into the hall of fame in 2000. Two years later, computer inventors J. Presper Eckert Jr. and John Mauchly were inducted.

- Douglas Engelbart invented the computer mouse in 1963–1964. It had one button and a carved wooden casing. At a 1968 conference, he presented it as an "X-Y Position Indicator for a Display System."

- Charles Babbage is often credited as one of the first computer inventors. His Analytical Engine had all the elements of a modern automatic computer. This included storage, memory, and an input and output device. It was never built in his lifetime. However, it led to Augusta Ada King, the Countess of Lovelace, becoming the world's first computer programmer. She designed sequences of instructions for the Analytical Engine.

Starting with ABC

The Atanasoff-Berry Computer (ABC) was the first electronic **digital** computer. Built in 1939, the ABC was the size of a large desk. It weighed 700 pounds (318 kg)! The ABC amazed everyone. It had the ability to solve 29 **equations** at once.

But the ABC was only the beginning. Faster machines were already being designed. By 1944, the Harvard Mark I had been revealed.

The Harvard Mark I was the first **automatic** digital computer. It weighed 10,000 pounds (4,500 kg)! And, it solved equations up to 23 digits wide. This was another big step in the history of computers.

By 1945, another monster machine was built. This was the Electronic Numerical Integrator and Computer, or ENIAC. ENIAC was built for use in **World War II**. Luckily, it was a general-purpose electronic digital computer. So after the war, ENIAC could be used for a variety of mathematical problems.

J. Presper Eckert Jr. and John William Mauchly invented ENIAC at the University of Pennsylvania. It was 1,000 times faster than the Mark I.

Even while ENIAC was in use, improvements were being made. The Electronic Discrete Variable **Automatic** Computer (EDVAC) was ready in 1951. EDVAC had a big advantage over previous devices. It could hold more information from one use to the next.

Next, the makers of ENIAC and EDVAC designed a new machine. They invented the Universal Automatic Computer (UNIVAC) in 1951. Unlike previous computers, a UNIVAC could work equally well with numbers and letters. It was used by the U.S. **Census** Bureau. A UNIVAC also correctly **predicted** the 1952 U.S. presidential election.

UNIVAC was a commercial success. Forty-six were sold during the 1950s.

Computers continued to improve rapidly. The invention of the supercomputer came next. Supercomputers can be made up of hundreds of powerful **microprocessors** working together. They help with impressive work, from designing airplanes to studying weather patterns.

As of 2007, the world's fastest supercomputer was IBM's BlueGene/L. It performed at 280.6 teraflops. One teraflop is equal to one trillion calculations per second!

IBM's BlueGene/L is located at the Lawrence Livermore National Laboratory in California.

Young Inventors

Bill Gates (left) *began creating software with Paul Allen* (right) *when he was just 15 years old. Today, Gates is one of the world's wealthiest people.*

Numerous inventors contributed to the computers we use today. American professor John V. Atanasoff is an important inventor of the modern computer. In 1939, Atanasoff and his assistant Clifford E. Berry built the ABC.

Another young computer wizard gained attention in the 1970s. William "Bill" Henry Gates III left Harvard University to create **software**. In 1975, Gates and his friend Paul G. Allen cofounded Microsoft Corporation.

The same year, the first personal computer (PC) was introduced. Microsoft soon produced software for these popular new machines. Today, Microsoft remains a leader in the computer world.

Next, Steven P. Jobs entered the scene. In 1976, Jobs cofounded Apple Computer Inc. with Stephen G. Wozniak.

Steven P. Jobs

The following year, the company produced the popular Apple II. In 1983, it simplified computer use with the Apple Lisa. This was the first commercial computer to use a mouse. In 1984, it created the Macintosh. The Apple Lisa and the Macintosh also used **icons**.

Bits and Pieces

A motherboard is a computer's main circuit board. The CPU, memory chips, and chips that control peripheral devices are all connected to it.

A computer's central processing unit (CPU) acts like its brain. In reality, the CPU is a **microprocessor chip** that turns information into results.

Part of the CPU is called the control unit. It interprets instructions given to the computer. Then, it passes the information to the proper part of the computer.

An operating system (OS) manages a computer's many processes. The OS makes the **internal** and **external** commands work together.

Memory chips store information on the computer. **Data** is stored on and retrieved from the hard drive. The hard drive is made of several important parts. These include magnetic discs and an arm with read/write heads.

Data is also stored **externally**. Common removable storage devices include compact discs (CDs) and **digital** video discs (DVDs). Other external storage devices include floppy disks and flash drives.

A computer takes instructions from **software**. OS software runs a computer's memory and manages data. Applications software helps with tasks such as word processing.

Read/write heads are on each side of a hard drive's magnetic discs, or platters. They store and retrieve information the computer needs.

16

Laptop ports are often located along one side of the computer. Power cords, peripheral devices, and even flash drives can be plugged in there.

Computers also have **hardware** such as **peripheral** devices. These devices are added on to expand a computer's capabilities. They usually connect to a computer by a cable and plug into a **port**.

A printer is one example of a peripheral device. It takes commands from your computer. Then, it makes a hard copy of your work.

A keyboard is another peripheral device. It is used to type text and edit documents. The keyboard is often used together with a mouse.

A computer tracks the movements of a mouse. This moves a **cursor** on the screen. Users click the mouse when the cursor is on an **icon**. This tells the computer to do the icon's task. The mouse can drag items across a screen. It can also open menus to use other programs.

Icons, menus, cursors, and the mouse make up the graphical user interface (GUI). The GUI helps make computers user-friendly.

A computer screen is called a monitor. The monitor is where you can see the results of your work. It even allows users to watch movies and play games!

An internal ball or a light tracks a mouse's movements. That information is sent to a microprocessor in the computer. This tells the cursor how to move.

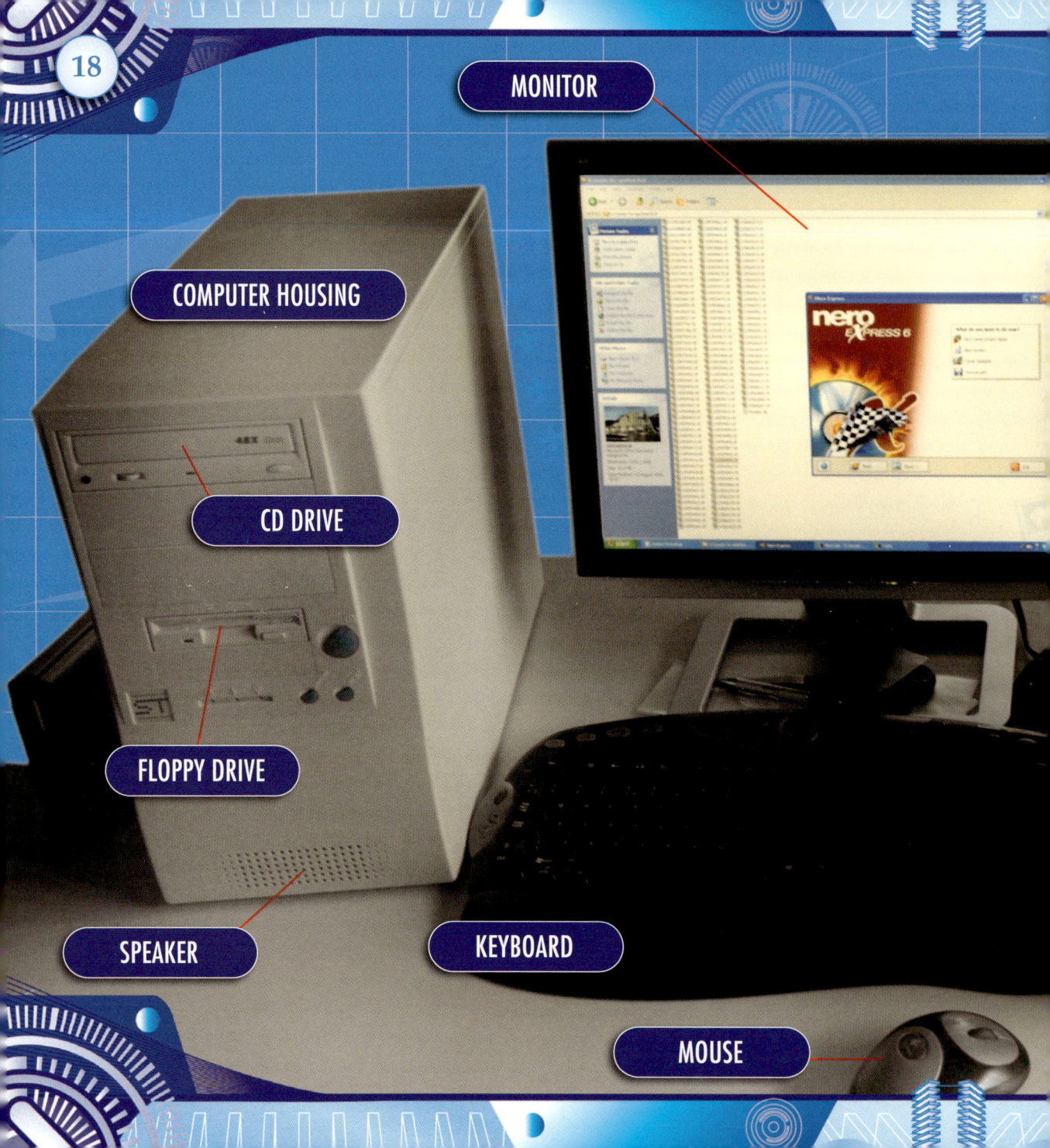

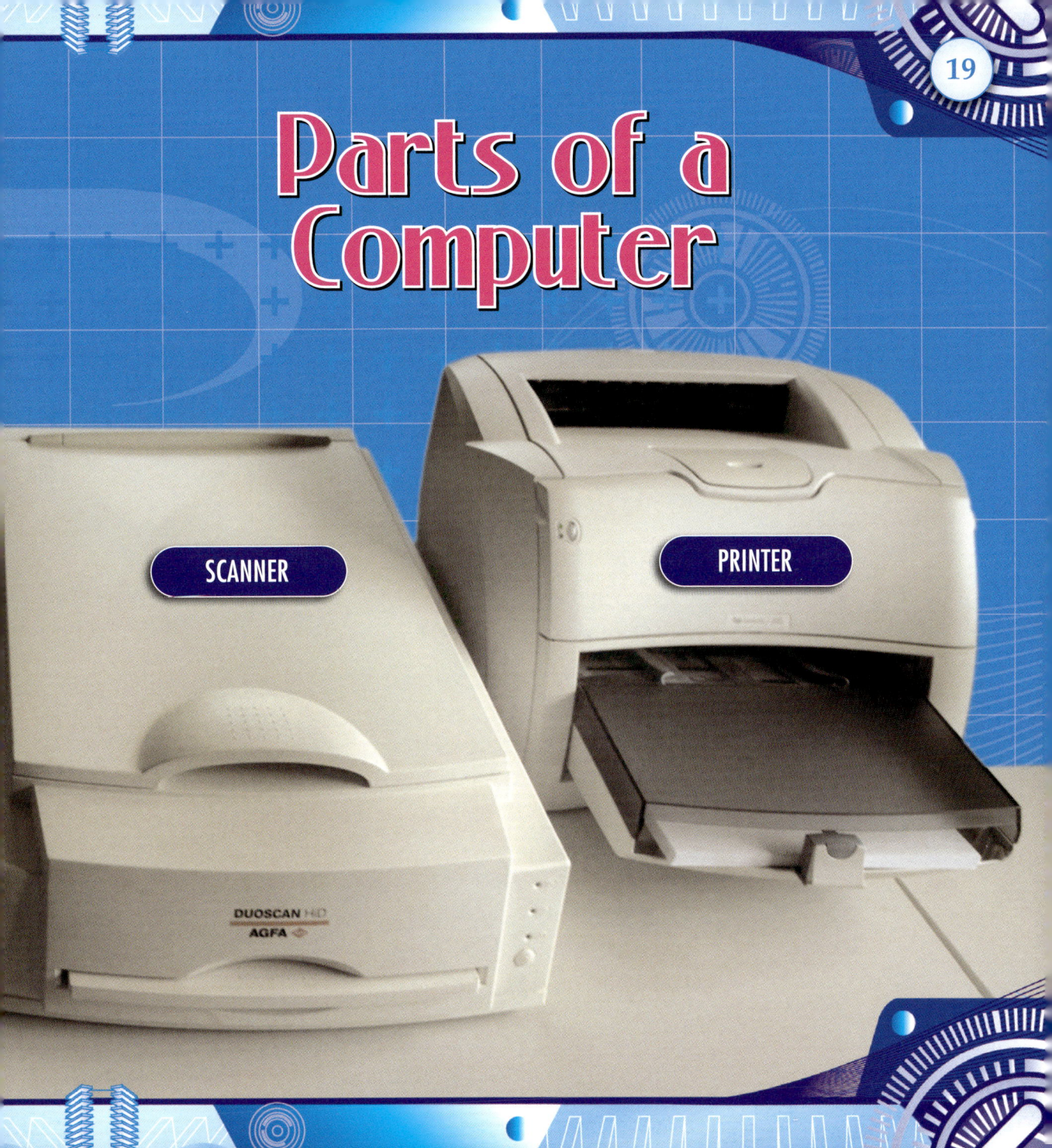

Input and Output

Computers come preloaded with some **software**. For example, these machines just wouldn't work without an OS! These basic **internal** programs allow a computer to run.

Computers then have the ability to take in information from outside sources. This is called input. It can come from you. This could be through devices such as a mouse or a keyboard. It can also come from storage devices. These include CD drives and flash drives.

Input goes to the CPU. The CPU works with this information to produce results. These results can be saved in the memory for later use. Or, they can be sent to output or storage devices.

A desktop computer's housing holds its internal components, or parts. It also provides connections for external devices.

INSIDE A COMPUTER

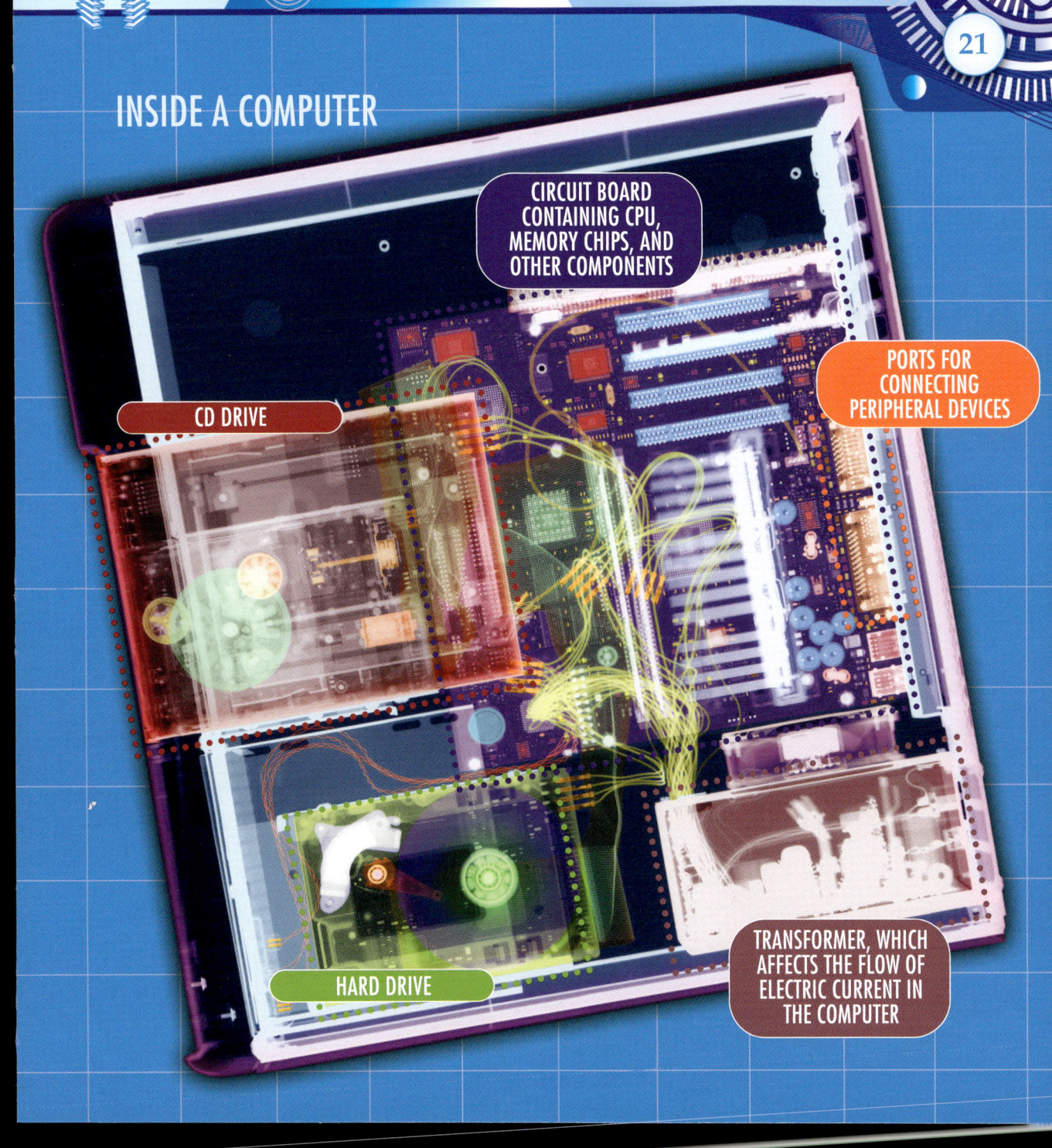

Digital World

Most modern computers are **digital**, rather than **analog** or **hybrid**. PCs and Apple's Macintosh computers are extremely popular digital personal computers. They are designed for general use by individuals like you. Desktops, laptops, and handheld computers are all examples of personal

With a power cord or a fully charged battery, you can use a laptop anywhere!

computers. Desktops are large. As their name implies, they are not meant to be carried around.

Laptops and notebooks are meant to be carried! Despite their smaller size, they can be just as powerful as desktops. Every required computer part is in these book-sized machines. That includes the hard drive and the keyboard. Another advantage of laptops is their ability to operate on battery power.

Personal **digital** assistants (PDAs) are a type of handheld computer. These tiny devices are small enough to hold in your palm. Often, they cannot run as many programs as desktops or laptops. However, many PDAs can access e-mail and keep track of appointments. They can even work as cellular telephones!

Instead of a keyboard, many handheld computers use a touch screen. Users write on it with a special pen called a stylus.

Networking

Most types of computers are great for word processing and playing games. But connecting computers in a network adds to the amazing things they can do!

A network of computers is often connected to a server. A server is a central computer that provides services to other devices.

Servers are powerful and are usually found in businesses. They act as storage units and help computers share information on the network. Servers may also control shared **peripheral** devices, such as printers.

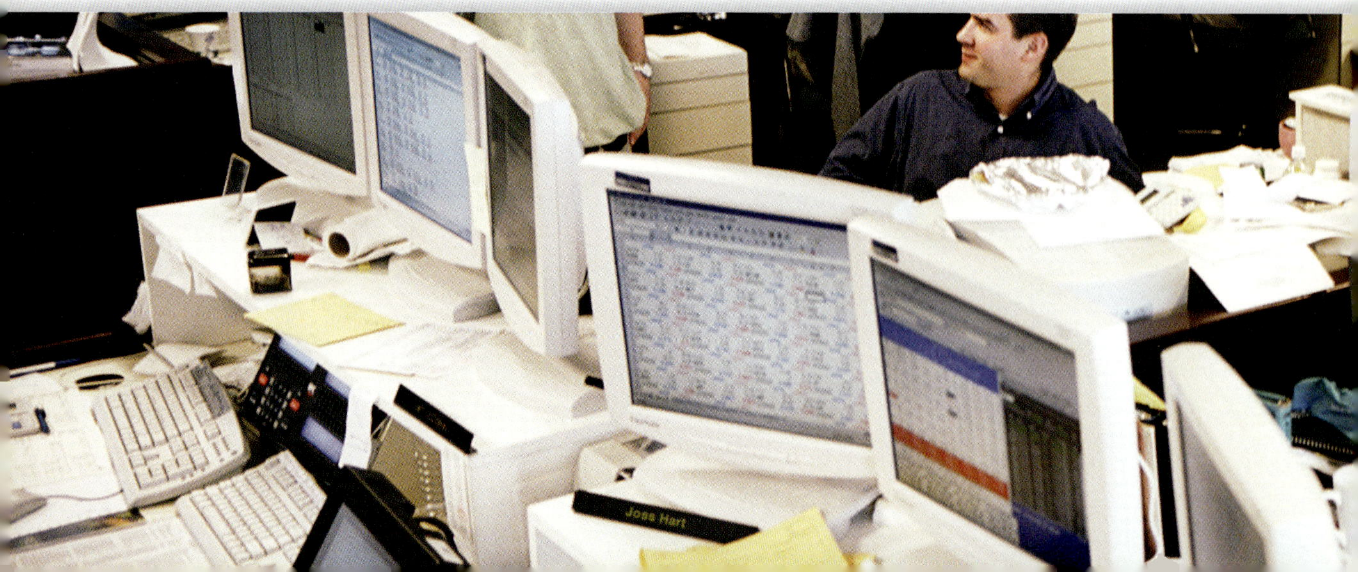

This networking trend began with the Advanced Research Projects Agency Network (ARPANet). The U.S. Department of Defense created ARPANet. Starting in 1969, ARPANet connected university and government computers. That way, they could share information in case of war.

Today, millions of computers are connected to the Internet. The Internet is like a system of networks. It is used not just by one company, but by the world!

The Internet allows computer users to communicate globally. In 1991, this became easier with the World Wide Web. And in 1993, **software** called browsers made the Internet even easier to navigate.

Office computers are connected to each other through a network and a server. This allows workers to easily share and access the same information.

High-Tech Work

If you love computers, you may want to work with them one day. You can turn your passion for computer games into a career. Computer game designers make those awesome games you play! They work with teams of artists, writers, and programmers.

Programmers have very important jobs. They translate instructions into a computer language, or code. This code tells the computer what to do.

Maybe you're more interested in computer guts than in games. If so, there's work for you too. Service professionals must understand a computer's many parts. And, they must know how to fix them if something goes wrong. There is an added bonus to this profession. Someone who fixes computers is a hero!

If you love having the latest gadgets, you might enjoy selling computers. Salespeople keep on top of trends and new equipment. They use their knowledge to help customers find just the right computer.

Books, Web sites, and computer experts can help you learn how to build and repair computers yourself!

Computer Culture

Computers impact our daily lives. They help us with homework and business. Computers bring us news and weather updates. They also make it easy to keep in touch with friends and family.

Even when we're not sitting in front of one, computers affect us. They are more than just the desktop versions most people use. There are computers in cars, airplanes, **satellites**, and even wristwatches! Today, these devices are everywhere.

This invention also has drawbacks. For example, being able to quickly share information can affect a person's privacy. Also, people may use these machines to commit crimes. A responsible adult should help younger computer users avoid these dangers.

Luckily, the positive impact far outweighs the negative. This amazing invention will continue to grow and improve. The future of computers is exciting and unstoppable!

Make sure an adult always knows when and how you're using a computer. That way, this important invention will remain entertaining, educational, and safe!

GLOSSARY

analog - of or relating to something that uses measurable physical quantities, such as weight or length, rather than numbers.
automatic - something that happens by itself, without anyone's control.
census (SEHNT-suhs) - a count of the population of a certain area.
chip - also called an integrated circuit. It is an arrangement of electronic components and their connections on a tiny piece of material such as silicon.
cursor - a visual, movable symbol used to mark a position, as on a computer screen.
data - information, often in numerical form.
digital - of or relating to numerical data that can be read by a computer.
equation - a mathematical statement showing equality between two elements, often using an equal sign. A statement such as 1 + 1 = 2 is an equation.
external - of, relating to, or being on the outside.
hardware - the physical equipment that makes up a computer system.
hybrid - combining two or more functions or ways of operation. For example, hybrid computers combine analog and digital computer systems.
icon - a symbol, such as on a computer screen, that represents a certain function or purpose.
internal - of, relating to, or being on the inside.
microprocessor - a type of computer program contained on an integrated-circuit chip.

peripheral (puh-RIH-fuh-ruhl) - of or relating to a device connected to a computer.
port - a connection where external devices are attached to a computer.
predict - to declare in advance.
satellite - a manufactured object that orbits Earth.
software - the written computer programs used in a computer.
World War II - from 1939 to 1945, fought in Europe, Asia, and Africa. Great Britain, France, the United States, the Soviet Union, and their allies were on one side. Germany, Italy, Japan, and their allies were on the other side.

WEB SITES

To learn more about computers, visit ABDO Publishing Company on the World Wide Web at **www.abdopublishing.com**. Web sites about computers are featured on our Book Links page. These links are routinely monitored and updated to provide the most current information available.

INDEX

A
Allen, Paul G. 13
Apple Computer Inc. 13, 22
Apple Lisa 13
Apple II 13
Atanasoff, John V. 12
Atanasoff-Berry Computer 8, 12

B
Berry, Clifford E. 12
BlueGene/L 11

C
careers 26, 27
central processing unit 14, 20
CD 15
CD drive 20
cursor 17

D
DVD 15
desktop computer 22, 23, 28

E
Electronic Discrete Variable Automatic Computer 10
Electronic Numerical Integrator and Computer 8, 10

F
flash drive 15, 20
floppy disk 15

G
Gates, William Henry, III 13
graphical user interface 17

H
handheld computer 22, 23
hard drive 14, 15, 23
Harvard Mark I 8

I
icons 13, 17
Internet 5, 25

J
Jobs, Steven P. 13

K
keyboard 16, 20, 23

L
laptop computer 22, 23

M
Macintosh 13, 22
memory 14, 15, 20
microprocessor 10, 14
Microsoft Corporation 13
monitor 17
mouse 13, 16, 17, 20

N
network 24, 25
notebook computer 23

O
operating system 14, 15, 20

P
port 16
printer 16, 24

S
server 24
software 13, 15, 20, 25
supercomputer 10, 11

U
Universal Automatic Computer 10

W
Wozniak, Stephen G. 13